This document is geared towards providing exact and reliable information in regards to the topic and issue covered. The publication is sold with the idea that the publisher is not required to render accounting, officially permitted, or otherwise, qualified services. If advice is necessary, legal or professional, a practiced individual in the profession should be ordered.

Under no circumstance will any legal responsibility or blame be held against the publisher for any reparation, damages, or monetary loss due to the information herein, either directly or indirectly.

Legal Notice:

The book is copyright protected. This is only for personal use. You cannot amend, distribute, sell, use, quote or paraphrase any part or the content within this book without the consent of the author.

Disclaimer Notice:

Please note the information contained within this document is for educational and entertainment purposes only. Every attempt has been made to provide accurate, up to date and reliable complete information. No warranties of any kind are expressed or implied. Readers acknowledge that the author is not engaging in the rendering of legal, financial, medical or professional advice. The content of this book has been derived from various sources. Please consult a licensed professional before attempting any techniques outlined in this book.

By reading this document, the reader agrees that under no circumstances are is the author responsible for any loses, direct or indirect, which are incurred as a result the use of information contained within this document, including, but not limited to, —errors, omissions, or inaccuracies.

INTRODUCTION

The world is obsessed about health as we have learnt that good health is the prime key for good life. Good health comes from healthy living and most importantly, healthy food. Nutritionists and doctors all over the world are busy in finding out the best food habit and in the attempt; they are keen about finding out the things which can cause harm to us. In this attempt, the slightest threat imposing ingredients and materials are being marked as harmful and immediate remedy is being sought out. Today we are going to talk about one such thing which has been found to be harmful for the health and is thus the most popular talking topic in the world of nutrition and health.

Yes, we are talking about Lectin. Lectin is a type of plant protein that is necessary for the growth of the plant. Certain scientists believe that lectins are efficient in creating a defence mechanism for the plants to keep the insects away. Clinical study on this particular nutrient reveals that it is rich in nitrogen; hence the fact behind its role as a growth nutrient for plants becomes clear. As far as the effect of lectins in human body is concerned, it is found that it helps human cells to interact with one another. But it has also been found that lectins have great impact on our health in multiple ways. It has been found that lectins cause digestion diseases, clustering tendency in red blood cells and certain other chronic diseases. Scientists have found out that lectins often act as anti-nutrients (i.e. the ones which block the absorption of other necessary nutrients). Lectins are present in several parts of the plant body and most of them are found in the seeds (since the seeds need major protection and good growth), and sadly, it is the seed that we mostly consume. We also prefer certain dishes (like salads) made with uncooked vegetables and used to nurture the idea that uncooked vegetables are extremely good (as compared to the cooked ones) as the nutrients are not tampered due to heat and using of spices or oil. Now, this is where the entire world of nutrition turns upside down as we now come to know that presence of lectin is the cause of stomach upset when vegetables (especially legumes) are consumed raw or undercooked. We had known red kidney beans to be a great nutrient provider, but the presence of high amount of lectin in this particular legume was not known to us. Now, when we come to know about it – we feel greatly scared!!! Phytohaemagglutinin is the name of the lectin found in red kidney beans and this one is the culprit for causing red kidney bean poisoning due to consumption of undercooked beans. Doctors have revealed another frightening fact that consumption of only four raw red kidney beans can cause life-threatening poisoning including severe nausea, diarrhoea and vomiting.

Feeling scared???? You must be.....but we are just discussing the facts and it is foolish to close your eyes from the facts and keep on walking on the dangerous road instead of knowing the truth to stay safe. Now, the good news is that cooking is the best way to get rid of lectins from your food. Cooking methods which use moist heat are helpful in reducing the quantity of lectins from plant products. Not just moist cooking, it is the cooking process that breaks down plant starch into simpler carbohydrates and the lectins prefer to attach with such carbohydrates and thus can be removed from our body. We must also mention here that cooking has to be done in high temperature so that the lectins present in plant based ingredients can be eliminated only when they are cooked on high heat. Other methods of reducing the amount of lectins are boiling, fermentation, sprouting, peeling, deseeding and pressure cooking.

All You Need to Know About Lectin-Free Diet:

Lectin-Free diet is nothing but limiting or eliminating the intake of lectin. Well, this is a new nutrition trend and has recently been popularized by Dr. Steven Gundry. He is a former heart surgeon who later switched his field of work to food and supplement-based medicines. According to Dr. Gundry, lectin is one of the primary dangers found in the diet of majority of the Americans. His book on this subject provides all the vital information regarding the methods of avoiding lectin, the alternative food choices as well as the recipes. Dr. Gundry also mentions that a lectin-free diet can be of great help as far as weight reduction is concerned.

To be precise, the benefits of lectin free diet are manifold. According to several nutrition scientists and medical practitioners around the world, lectins are known to cause inflammation, autoimmune disease, diabetes and rheumatoid arthritis. Especially the wheat germ lectin is associated with disturbance in the immune system due to increased inflammation. Long term inflammation can lead to life-threatening diseases like heart disease, depression and even cancer. Following a lectin-free or reduced-lectin diet can help in lowering the inflammation in the body. Research shows evidences that it becomes easier for the bacteria or other harmful toxins to go through the gut barrier in the presence of lectin. This implies your body will stay safe from harmful bacteria and toxins when you consume lesser amounts of lectins.

The Opposite Side of the Coin:

Having said that food products like whole grains are extremely rich in lectins, it is obvious that those foods have been put at the top of the 'banned' list for lectin free diet. But how can we ignore the fact that whole grains contain high amounts of antioxidants; which is one of the most effective nutrients in fighting against inflammation? So, it turns up like that – the food we are rejecting due to the presence of lectin in it (read the outer coating of the grain contains maximum amount of lectin) is internally rich in the nutrient which is most important in fighting the disease or condition caused for consuming lectins.

What to do? Find the best middle path which will help in keeping perfect balance for a healthy diet. Moreover, any strict diet plan is not just hard but almost impossible to follow for common people. You can maintain the strict lectin-free diet for a short time, but when you go for long-term; it is pretty impossible feast to achieve. A complete lectin free diet actually cuts you off from several nutritious foods such as the whole grains, beans and many vegetables. Just talking about the whole grains; which is rich in nutrients which help in fighting against cardiac conditions, cancer and diabetes – it is not wise to eliminate them totally from the diet. The way out is to maintain a good balance and at the same time making sure that whatever grain you eat, reduce the amount of lectin from it.

So…..What to eat and what to Avoid?

According to Dr. Gundry, you can go for the following foods when you desire to limit the intake of lectins.

- Pasture raised meat – this is great option to make sure you have enough protein in your diet.
- Casein A2 milk – you must avoid Casein A1 milk completely.
- Sweet potatoes – though potatoes are rich in lectin, the sweet potato is great for lectin free diet. You will get greater health benefits when you consume cooked sweet potatoes.

- Cruciferous vegetables – broccoli, Brussels sprout, cauliflower are the vegetables which are sure to give you great nutrients and at the same time they are very low in lectin content.
- Asparagus
- Celery
- Mushroom – you can choose from the wide varieties of mushroom.
- Avocado – though it is a fruit, you can enjoy avocados in lectin free diet recipes.
- Olive and olive oil – olives are low in lectin content and thus safe to consume when you are on strict lectin free diet.

If you are trying to avoid lectins, you must stay away from the following foods:

- Any types of legumes like beans, peas, lentils and peanuts.
- Squash
- All the nightshade vegetables like eggplant, tomatoes, peppers and potatoes. However, tomato is one such vegetable which seems to be indispensable in cooking and keeping it away from your dish will mean finding hard-to-make substitute ingredients. Nutrition experts have thus recommended reducing the amount of lectins in the tomato by thoroughly peeling and deseeding them before using. In this book we have made use of tomatoes in several recipes and have thus mentioned using of reduced-lectin tomatoes.
- Fruits. But you cannot eliminate fruits completely from your diet. It will be foolish to say no to all fruits as they are super rich in healthy nutrients like minerals and vitamins. The best way to deal this issue is to go for in-season fruits and that too in moderation.

- Grains. If you need to consume grains, you must choose products made from white flour instead of the common wheat flour as it is the wheat flour that has greater amounts of lectins.
- Corn. This plant product must be completely avoided while you are on lectin free diet. Actually, you cannot reduce the amount of lectin in corn and thus best if left for normal diet.

How to Reduce Lectins from Your Diet?

We have already mentioned that fact that it is hard (read almost impossible) to follow the strict lectin free diet. It is however easy to follow the regime with reduced lectin foods. In that way you can enjoy the other goodness of plant products and at the same time stay safe from the harmful effects of lectin. Here are some tips to reduce the amounts of lectin from the foods we consume.

- Pressure cooking – Pressure cooking has always been the most healthy way of cooking as far as preservation of nutrients are concerned. However, as far as lectins are concerned, the pressure cooker just performs the opposite task. Pressure cooking actually destroys the amount of lectins present in plant products. If you are cooking beans, tomatoes, potatoes or quinoa in the pressure cooker, you are actually destroying the lectins present in them. It must be remembered that lectins present in wheat, oats, rye or barley cannot be destroyed by pressure cooking and thus, these foods must be rejected completely while on lectin free diet.
- Peeling and Deseeding – Majority of vegetables and fruits have the highest concentration of lectins in their skin and seeds. It is thus advised to peel and

deseed the fruits and vegetables thoroughly to reduce the amounts of lectin present in them. We have already mentioned the method of reducing lectin from tomatoes. You can do the same with other fruits and vegetables of your choice. Most fruits and vegetables are easy to peel. If they are not, just boil them and put in cold bath so that the peel comes off easily.

- Choose white instead of brown– Healthy food habits spoke of choosing brown grains instead of white. Now, we are on the lectin free diet and it advises just the opposite. You are generally advised to avoid grains, but if you must eat grains, choose the white ones – like have white rice instead of brown rice. Go for white bread instead of brown bread and so on.

A Note for The Book:

In this book we have compiled the recipes which can be made easily with easily available ingredients. We understand that certain cooking ingredients (read tomatoes) are indispensible and cannot be substituted easily. So we have made best efforts to share the tricks to reduce the amount of lectins in such ingredients. Hope the recipes will help you in achieving the perfect lectin free diet.

Top 100 Lectin Free Recipes

1. Tomato Wonder Sauce For Lectin-Free Diet

Total time: 2 hours 30 minutes

Servings: 2 cups

Ingredients:

- 5 tomatoes
- salt and black pepper
- 4 red chillies
- 1 cup chopped onion
- 1 tbsp olive oil
- ¼ tsp oregano

Directions:

Cut an X mark at the base of the tomatoes and boil them in salted water for 25 minutes and then put them in a cold bath. Peel off the skin and then cut them into wedges. Remove all the seeds and then put them in the blender along with onion and chilli. Run the device to make a smooth paste.

Heat olive oil in the crock pot and put the tomato mixture into the pot. Add salt, black pepper and oregano and stir well. Cover the pot and cook on low setting for 2 hours. Check for the desired consistency of the sauce and cook for some more time without the lid if required.

Let the sauce cool down completely before storing in air tight containers.

2. Lectin Free Shredded Pork

Total time: 18 hrs 30 mins

Servings: 5

Ingredients:

- 2 lb pork roast
- 9 oz homemade barbeque sauce
- 1½ large onions
- ½ cup ginger ale

Directions:

Slice the onion and keep half portion of them at the bottom of the crock pot and then keep the pork roast on top. Cover the roast with the remaining onion slices. Make a mixture with ginger ale and barbeque sauce and pour it into the crock pot.

Cover the pot and cook on low setting for 12 hours. Remove the meat and reserve the onion separately for later use. Discard all the cooking liquid and then shred the meat using forks.

Bring back the shredded meat into the crock pot and place the onion slices over the meat. Cover the pot and cook on low setting for another 6 hours.

Serve the pork warm with some more barbeque sauce.

3. Healthy Spinach Soup With Bliss of Turkey

Total time: 8 hrs

Servings: 4

Ingredients:

- 4 cups baby spinach
- 1 tbsp oregano
- 1 tbsp minced ginger
- 1 cup turkey meat, boiled and cubed
- Salt
- red chilli flakes

Directions:

Keep the turkey meat aside and then put all the other ingredients in the crock pot and cover them with just enough water. Close the lid and cook on low setting for 7 hours.

Let the soup sit for some time before opening the lid. Use an immersion blender to make the smooth soup and pour the liquid back to the pot.

Now, add the cooked turkey cubes and cook for another hour. Stir the soup thoroughly and serve hot by adding some more seasoning.

4. Lectin Free Chicken Taco

Total time: 6 hrs

Servings: 8

Ingredients:

- 1 lb chicken breast
- 1 cup chicken broth
- 3 tbsp taco seasoning

Directions:

Mix the taco seasoning in the chicken broth and keep aside.

Grease the crock pot with cooking spray and then place the chicken breast in the pot. Pour the mixture over the meat and then cover the pot.

Cook on medium setting for 6 hours and then let the chicken stand in the pot for some time. Open the lid and shred the chicken with two forks.

Serve the chicken warm with some boiled sweet potatoes and your favourite sauce.

5. Lectin Free Soup With Sausage

Total time: 6 hrs 5 mins

Servings: 4

Ingredients:

- 1 cup chopped onion
- 1 cup sautéed sausages, cubed
- 2 tbsp ginger, minced
- Salt
- red chilli flakes
- 3 cups mushroom stock

Directions:

Keep all the ingredients in the crock pot and close the lid. Cook on low setting for 6 hours and then let the soup sit in the pot for some time.

Stir the soup thoroughly and cook for another 5 minutes without the lid to get the right consistency of the soup.

Serve hot by seasoning with some more seasonings if required.

6. Healthy Chard Soup

Total time: 3 hrs 5 mins

Servings: 4

Ingredients:

- 2.5 cups chopped Swiss Chard
- 2 tbsp minced ginger
- 1 cup chopped onion
- 1 tsp oregano
- Salt
- red chilli flakes

Directions:

Keep all the ingredients in the crock pot and cover them with just enough water. Seal the pot and cook on medium setting for 3 hours.

When the cooking time is up, let the soup sit in the pot for some time and then open the lid. Use an immersion blender to make the soup smooth and creamy. Stir the soup thoroughly once again and serve hot by adding some more seasoning.

7. Super Cheesy Artichoke Frittata

Total time: 3 hrs 5 mins

Servings: 8

Ingredients:

- 8 eggs
- 4 oz feta cheese, crumbled
- ¼ cup very thinly sliced sweet potato
- ¼ cup green onion, sliced
- 1 tsp all-purpose seasoning
- 14 oz artichoke hearts, chopped
- 12 oz reduced-lectin tomatoes, roasted
- black pepper
- 2 tbsp parsley, chopped
- Salt

Directions:

Grease crock pot with olive oil and keep aside.

Put artichoke hearts and sweet potato at the bottom of the crock pot and then make a layer with sliced green onions. Put the eggs in a bowl and add ground black pepper and salt. Pour this mixture into the pot and use a fork to stir the contents gently. Make sure that the egg mixture is well distributed and the vegetables are well covered with it.

Cover the pot with a foil followed by the pot cover. Cook for 3 hours on low setting check if the egg is well set. Slice the frittata and garnish with parsley.

8. Soup-of-Cauliflower For Lectin Free Diet

Total time: 3 hrs 5 mins

Servings: 4

Ingredients:

- 1 tbsp ginger, minced
- 1 tsp lemon juice
- 3 cups cauliflower florets
- ½ tsp hot sauce
- Salt
- red chilli flakes

Directions:

Keep all the ingredients in the crock pot and cover them with 2 cups of water. Put on the lid of the pot and cook on medium setting for 3 hours.

Let the soup sit in the pot for some time after cooking and then open the lid. Use an immersion blender to make the soup smooth and creamy. Stir the soup thoroughly once again and serve hot by adding some more seasoning.

9. Crockpot Special Duck Roast

Total time: 2 hrs 10 mins

Servings: 6

Ingredients:

- 1 envelope dry vegetable soup mix
- 2 lb duck roast
- 1 large onion
- 1½ cups chicken broth
- 1½ cups sweet potato cubes

Directions:

Grease the crock pot with cooking spray and then place the duck roast at the bottom of the pot. Blend the soup mixture with the chicken broth and keep it aside.

Cut the onion into quarters and then pull them apart.

Place the vegetables around the meat and then pour the soup mixture over the top. Cover the pot and cook on high setting for 2 hours and then let the meat sit in the pot for some time.

Open the lid and serve the meat warm.

10. Lectin Free Creamy Chicken

Total time: 7 hrs 5 mins

Servings: 6

Ingredients:

- 1 envelope dry onion soup mix
- 1 lb boneless chicken breast
- 10 oz cream of mushroom soup
- 16 oz sour cream

Directions:

Grease the crock pot and place the chicken at the bottom.

Mix all the other ingredients thoroughly in a bowl and then pour the entire liquid over the chicken in the pot.

Cook on low setting for 7 hours and then open the lid.

Serve the chicken warm.

11. Super Pork Ribs For Lectin Free Diet

Total time: 9 hrs 10 mins

Servings: 4

Ingredients:

- 2 lb pork ribs
- 2/3 cup barbecue sauce
- 1 medium onion, sliced
- 1/3 cup plum jam
- 3 garlic cloves, minced

Directions:

Slice the onion and coat eh crock pot with olive oil. Place the pork ribs at the bottom of the pot and keep the garlic and onion slices over the meat. Cook on low setting for 8 hours and make sure that the meat is tender. Drain all the cooking juices and then return the meat and vegetables to the pot.

Mix the remaining ingredients and pour it over the meat in the pot. Shake the pot to coat the meat thoroughly with the juices and then cover to cook for another hour on low setting.

Simmer the meat for some time without the cover to get the right consistency of the gravy and then serve the pork as a side dish.

12.Healthy Apple Stew

Total time: 4 hrs 20 mins

Servings: 4

Ingredients:

- 3 lb apples
- A pinch of ground nutmeg
- 2 drops of stevia
- 1 tsp cinnamon
- 3 tbsp grass fed butter

Directions:

Slice the apples and then put all the ingredients in the crock pot.

Cook on low setting for 4 hours and open the lid immediately after cooking. The apple slices must be soft but not mushy.

You can serve the apples with ice cream.

13. Crock Pot Baked Dish – Super Apple

Total time: 4 hrs 15 mins

Servings: 5

Ingredients:

- 5 medium apples
- ½ tsp nutmeg powder
- ½ tsp cinnamon powder
- 2 drops of stevia
- 1 cup walnuts

Directions:

Peel the apples about a fourth of the way down and remove the cores and seeds.

Blend all the other ingredients in a bowl and fill the peeled apples with this mixture.

Coat the crock pot and the outside of the apples with butter and then place them in the crock pot.

Cook on low setting for 4 hours and then remove the lid immediately to avoid over cooking.

Let the apples cool down to room temperature and then serve by topping with cream of your choice.

14. Chicken Delight Egg Drop Soup

Total time: 3 hrs 10 mins

Servings: 4

Ingredients:

- 1 cup chicken cubes
- 1 large egg
- 1 tbsp ginger, minced
- 1 tbsp minced garlic
- Salt
- red chilli flakes
- 6 cups chicken broth

Directions:

Keep the egg aside and put all the ingredients in the crock pot and close the lid. Cook on low setting for 3 hours and then let the soup sit in the pot for some time.

Now, beat the egg with one tablespoon water and season it with salt. Pour out one cup of soup from the crock pot into a bowl and add this beaten egg into the soup. Remember to stir the soup constantly. The egg will set in a few minutes and will look like water drops. Pour the egg-mixture into the crock pot and cook for another 5 minutes. The soup must be very runny and you will serve it hot by adding seasonings as required.

15. Bacon & Spinach Blast Soup

Total time: 3 hrs 15 mins

Servings: 4

Ingredients:

- 3 cups baby spinach
- ½ cup sweet potato
- ½ cup broccoli florets
- 2 tbsp ginger and garlic, minced
- Salt
- red chilli flakes
- 3 bacon slices
- 3 cups vegetable broth

Directions:

Cook bacon slices in the crock pot till they become crispy. Keep them in a bowl for later use.

Use the leftover bacon grease from the pot and pour all the other ingredients into the pot and then close the lid. Cook on low setting for 3 hours and then let the soup sit in the pot for some time.

Now, crumble the crisped bacon slices and add them with the soup in the crock pot. Stir thoroughly and cook for another 5 minutes without the lid.

Check the seasoning and serve the soup hot.

16. Marvellous Crab Soup For Lectin Free Diet

Total time: 3 hrs 5 mins

Servings: 4

Ingredients:

- 1 cup cubed crab meat
- 1 tbsp minced garlic
- Salt
- red chilli flakes
- 3 cups vegetable broth
- 1 tsp lime juice

Directions:

Coat the crab cubes in lime juice and keep aside for some time.

Now, put all the ingredients in the crock pot and then close the lid. Cook on medium setting for 3 hours. Do not open the lid immediately after cooking. Let the soup sit for some time and then open the lid of the crock pot and simmer the soup for another 5 minutes without the lid to get the desired consistency of the soup.

Check the seasoning and serve the soup hot.

17. Delicious Bolognese Style Lamb

Total time: 8 hrs 5 mins

Servings: 4

Ingredients:

- 1 lb ground lamb
- 1 onion, chopped
- olive oil
- 2 garlic cloves, chopped
- ¾ cup vegetable stock
- ¼ tsp red chilli powder
- 1 medium sweet potato, finely chopped

Directions:

Heat oil in the crock pot to cook the lamb meat till the meat is no longer pink in colour. Now, add onion, garlic and sweet potato and cook for few more minutes.

Pour the vegetable stock and chilli powder and stir the meat thoroughly. Close the lid of the pot and cook on medium setting for 8 hours. Let the meat sit in the pot for some time and then open the lid.

Serve warm with cauliflower rice.

18. Lectin Free Chicken Hash

Total time: 8 hrs 5 mins

Servings: 4

Ingredients:

- 1 lb chicken, diced
- 1 cup chopped onion
- ½ cup chopped mushroom
- 4 tbsp grass-fed butter
- 1 cup diced sweet potatoes
- 4 oz water
- salt and red chilli flakes

Directions:

Sear the chicken thoroughly in the crock pot and then add butter, onion and mushroom. Sweat the vegetables and then add the sweet potatoes.

Add water and season with salt and red chilli flakes. Close the lid of the crock pot and cook on medium setting for 8 hours. Open the lid immediately and then serve the hash warm.

19. Lectin Free Super Herb Flavoured Beef

Total time: 8 hrs 10 mins

Servings: 4

Ingredients:

- 1 lb beef chunks
- 1.5 tbsp chopped thyme
- 1.5 tbsp chopped rosemary
- 3 garlic cloves, minced
- 2 cups beef stock
- salt
- olive oil

Directions:

Mix rosemary, thyme, salt and garlic and rub this mixture thoroughly over the beef chunks.

Heat olive oil in the crock pot and cook the meat till the chunks turn brown from all sides.

Close the lid and cook for 8 hours on high setting. Let the meat sit in the pot for few minutes and then open the lid.

Add beef stock in the pot and close the lid. Cook on manual setting for another 4 minutes and then open the lid immediately. Check if you have the right consistency of the gravy. Simmer if required and serve warm.

20. Coconut Flavoured Super Lamb

Total time: 8 hrs 5 mins

Servings: 8

Ingredients:

- 1 lb lamb cubes
- 1 cup chopped onion
- 1 garlic clove, minced
- 2 cups coconut milk
- ¼ cup coconut flour
- coconut oil

Directions:

Heat coconut oil in the crock pot and cook the lamb cubes till they turn brown. Cook the onion and garlic for few minutes and then add coconut flour, coconut milk and salt.

Cook on medium setting for 8 hours and then allow few minutes of standing time before opening the lid. Serve the gravy style lamb as a side dish with cauliflower rice.

21.Pork & Mushroom – Super Combo Hash

Total time: 3 hrs 5 mins

Servings: 4

Ingredients:

- 1 medium onion, chopped
- 1 tsp garlic paste
- 2 cups cooked chicken cubes
- 1 lb button mushroom
- 4 celery ribs, finely chopped
- 4 tbsp butter

Directions:

Heat the crock pot and sauté the mushrooms for a minute. Add butter, garlic paste, onion, chicken cubes and celery and sweat them for a couple of minutes.

Season the ingredients with salt and pepper. Close the lid of the pot and cook on medium setting for 3 hours. Let the hash sit in the pot for few minutes and then serve the dish warm.

22. Mustard Crowned Salmon For Lectin Free Diet

Total time: 2 hrs 5 mins

Servings: 4

Ingredients:

- 1.5 lb salmon fillets
- ¼ cup sour cream
- 2 tbsp mustard
- 2 tsp lime juice
- Salt
- red chilli flakes

Directions:

Cut the fish into four pieces and rub some lime juice over them.

Heat the crock pot and place the salmon fillets in the pot. Remember to keep the fish with the skin side down.

Blend all the other ingredients to make a smooth paste and spread the mixture with a spoon over the fish fillets. Close the pot and cook on high setting for 2 hours. Let the fish sit in the pot for two minutes before removing the lid.

Serve warm with lime wedges.

23. Super Fruity Bread

Total time: 3 hrs 5 mins

Servings: 16

Ingredients:

- ½ cup dried Mango cubes
- 1 tsp stevia powder
- ½ cup dried apricot
- 2 tsp baking powder
- ¼ cup pistachio nuts, chopped
- 1¾ cup almond flour
- 4 egg whites
- ½ cup apple juice
- ¼ tsp baking soda
- ¼ tsp ground allspice
- 1 tbsp vanilla extract
- 2 oz chopped almonds
- ½ cup melted butter
- ¼ tsp sea salt
- ½ cup goat milk yogurt
- 1 cup mango puree
- ¼ cup olive oil

Directions:

Grease the crock pot and line it with parchment paper. Keep the prepared pot aside for later use.

Put apple juice, dried mangoes, pistachio, and apricots in a pan and cook them on high heat to bring the mixture to a boil. Remove the pan from heat let the mixture cool down a bit.

Blend almond flour, stevia, baking soda, baking powder, ground allspice, and salt in a large mixing bowl.

Add the fruit mixture with mango puree, melted butter, vanilla extract, egg whites, yogurt, and olive oil and whisk hard to make a smooth mixture. Combine the dry and wet mixture thoroughly to make the batter. Pour the batter into the prepared crock pot and cover it with a foil. Now, add the dry mixture to this bowl and blend thoroughly to make a smooth batter. Pour the batter into the greased crock pot and make the top smooth with the help of a spoon. Now, cover the top with a foil tightly.

Close the lid and cook on high setting for 2 hours 45 minutes. Check for the doneness of the bread and serve after complete cooling.

24. Garlic Flavoured Broccoli Noodles

Total time: 3 hrs

Servings: 4

Ingredients:

- 4 large broccoli stems
- 1.5 tbsp lemon juice
- 1 tsp red chilli flakes
- 10 garlic cloves
- 1 tbsp olive oil

Directions:

Use size C spiralizer to make noodles from the broccoli stems. Cook the noodles in salt water till they become tender. Make sure not to overcook and make the noodles mushy.

Now, put olive oil in the crock pot and cook the garlic cloves for a minute. Add the chilli flakes and cook for another 1 hour. Add the cooked noodles along with lemon juice and toss the entire ingredients for some time.

Serve the noodles warm with your favourite side dish.

25. Power Breakfast From Crockpot

Total time: 5 hrs 30 mins

Servings: 4

Ingredients:

- 4 large eggs
- 1 cup broccoli florets
- ½ cup sweet potato cubes
- Salt
- Black pepper
- 1 cup water

Directions:

Place the eggs in inside the crock pot and pour enough water to cover the eggs completely.

Close the lid and cook on low setting for 3 hours and 30 minutes. Open the lid and let the eggs cool down a bit. Now, peel the eggs and keep them in a bowl.

Clean the crock pot and put the vegetables along with a cup of water. Season with salt and then let the vegetables cook on low setting for 2 hours. They must be tender but crispy.

Serve the hard boiled eggs with the steaming vegetables and remember to season with salt and black pepper.

26. Lectin Free Orange Cake (Egg-free Version)

Total time: 4 hrs 15 mins

Servings: 12

Ingredients:

- 1½ cups almond flour
- 1 cup dried oranges, chopped
- 1 tsp baking powder
- ½ tsp baking soda
- ½ cup goat yogurt
- 1 tsp liquid stevia

Directions:

Mix the wet and dry ingredients separately and then blend them together to make smooth batter.

Grease the crock pot with some butter and pour the cake batter into the pot. Cover with a towel to prevent the moisture from dripping on the cake. Cover the pot and bake on low setting for 4 hours.

Check if the cake is well set and then serve after cooling down.

27. Super Veggie Frittata

Total time: 3 hrs 5 mins

Servings: 6

Ingredients:

- 8 eggs
- 2 cups mixed vegetables (sweet potato, spinach, broccoli)
- ½ cup grated cheddar cheese
- 2 garlic cloves
- Salt and black pepper

Directions:

Keep all the ingredients in a bowl and whisk them hard to make the frittata batter. Line the crock pot with parchment paper and then pour the frittata batter inside the pot.

Cook on low setting for 3 hours and then open the lid. Remove the frittata along with the parchment paper and then place it in the oven to broil for 5 minutes and then serve warm.

28. Bliss Of Beef Balls With Veg-Noodles

Total time: 1 hr 5 mins

Servings: 4

Ingredients:

- 5 large cauliflower stems
- 10 garlic cloves
- 2 tsp red chilli flakes
- Baked beef balls
- ½ cup salsa sauce

Directions:

Use the size C spiralizer to make noodles from the cauliflower stems and cook them in salt water till they become tender but crispy.

Put some olive oil in the crock pot and cook the chilli flakes for half minute. Add the salsa sauce and cook for another hour. Add the cooked cauliflower noodles and toss for some time.

Now, add the baked beef balls and salsa sauce and then toss to coat the turkey balls and noodles with the salsa sauce.

Serve the dish warm.

29. Lectin Free Chicken Magic

Total time: 6 hrs 5 mins

Servings: 4

Ingredients:

- 1¼ lb boneless chicken fillets
- 2 tbsp mustard
- 2 tsp lemon juice
- ¼ cup sour cream
- Salt and black pepper

Directions:

Cut the chicken in four equal pieces and keep them inside the heated crock pot.

Prepare a smooth paste with mustard, lemon juice, cream, salt and pepper and spread the mixture with a spoon over the chicken fillets. Close the pot and cook on high pressure for 6 hours. Let the pressure release naturally before removing the lid.

Garnish with lime wedges.

30. Almond Magic Butter Chicken

Total time: 22 mins

Servings: 4

Ingredients:

- 1 tbsp melted butter
- 1 lb chicken breast
- 2 tbsp lime juice
- ½ tsp lime zest
- ¼ tsp chilli powder
- 2 tbsp toasted almonds

Directions:

Cook the chicken breasts in olive oil and remember to season the meat with salt and pepper and cook till the chicken turns slightly brown in colour. Close the lid and cook on low setting for 6 hours. Let the chicken sit in the pot for some time and then open the lid. Transfer the cooked chicken on the serving plate.

Make a mixture with melted butter, lime juice, lime zest and chilli powder and pour it over the cooked chicken.

Sprinkle the toasted almonds and serve the chicken warm.

31.Super Mushroom Breakfast For Lectin Free Diet

Total time: 4 hrs 40 mins

Servings: 2

Ingredients:

- 4 Portobello mushrooms
- 4 large eggs
- ½ cup shredded gouda cheese
- 2 cups cooked spinach
- ½ cup crumbled bacon

Directions:

Remove the stems of the mushrooms and then place them upside down on a plate.

Cook the spinach leaves in the crock pot with salt and water. Cook for 2 hours and then check if the leaves have wilted completely. Season the cooked spinach with salt and pepper and then divide them equally among the mushroom caps. Crack the eggs and pour one egg into each mushroom cap. Now, sprinkle the crisped bacon and shredded cheese.

Coat the crock pot with some butter and then keep the mushroom caps inside the pot. Close the lid and cook on low setting for 2 hours 30 minutes. Open the lid immediately to avoid over cooking.

Serve warm with sauce.

32. Omelette-de-Cheese (Lectin Free Recipe)

Total time: 3 hrs 5 mins

Servings: 4

Ingredients:

- 1 cup milk
- 8 eggs
- 1 cup sharp cheddar cheese
- Salt
- Black pepper

Directions:

Put all the ingredients in a bowl and whisk hard to make a frothy mixture.

Coat the crock pot with olive oil and pour the egg mixture into it. Close the pot and cook on low setting for 3 hours. Open the lid immediately and serve by garnishing with more cheese.

33. Blissful Coconutty Banana Cake

Total time: 4 hrs 15 mins

Servings: 12

Ingredients:

- 1½ cups coconut flour
- 1 tsp baking powder
- 5 eggs
- ½ cup coconut flakes
- 1 cup mashed ripe banana
- ½ cup goat yogurt
- 1 tsp liquid stevia

Directions:

Whisk the eggs hard and then add all the wet ingredients with it. blend the dry ingredients together and then mix the two mixtures to make the cake batter.

Coat the crock pot with butter and then pour the cake batter into the pot. Cover with a kitchen towel to avoid dripping of moisture on the cake.

Close the lid and cook on low setting for 4 hours. Let the cake sit in the pot for some time and then put on wire rack to cool it down completely.

Top with coconut cream and fresh banana slices.

34. Cheesy Crockpot Casserole With Beef

Total time: 3 hrs 5 mins

Servings: 12

Ingredients:

- 3 medium onion, chopped
- 2 garlic cloves, minced
- ½ tsp red chilli flakes
- 1 lb ground beef
- Olive oil
- 8 eggs
- 2 cups milk
- 2 cups mozzarella cheese

Directions:

Heat olive oil in a skillet and cook one onion and garlic till they become fragrant. Add the chilli flakes and beef and cook till the meat is thoroughly cooked. Let the meat cool down to room temperature.

Line the crock pot with parchment paper and then grease it thoroughly with butter.

Spread the cooked beef inside the pot and sprinkle chopped onion and cheese on top.

Beat the eggs and whisk with milk, salt and pepper. Pour this egg mixture over the beef and cheese in the pot. Close the lid of the crock pot and then cook on manual setting for 3 hours. Let the casserole sit in the pot for some time and then open the lid.

Bring out the casserole dish and serve by slicing into desired sizes.

35. Precious Parsley Delight Omelette

Total time: 25 mins

Servings: 4

Ingredients:

- 1 cup milk
- 2 tbsp freshly chopped parsley
- 1 cup grated gouda cheese
- 8 eggs
- Salt and black pepper

Directions:

Beat the eggs in a bowl and add the parsley and cheese with the egg. Remember to season eggs with salt and pepper.

Coat the crock pot with cooking spray and pour the egg mixture into it. Close the pot and cook on low setting for 3 hours. Open the lid immediately to ensure that the omelette remains super soft.

Slice the omelette into four pieces and serve by garnishing with some more cheese.

36. Sweet Potato Delight Hash

Total time: 3 hrs 5 mins

Servings: 4

Ingredients:

- 1 lb sweet potato, diced
- 2 cups cooked chicken cubes
- 4 celery ribs, finely chopped
- 1 medium onion, chopped
- 4 tbsp butter

Directions:

Heat the crock pot and cook the sweet potato dices for a minute. Add butter, onion, cooked chicken cubes and celery and sweat them for a couple of minutes.

Season the ingredients with salt and pepper. Close the lid of the pot and cook on low setting for 3 hours. Let the dish sit in the pot for 5 minutes and then serve the dish warm.

37. Coconut Bread For Lectin-Free Diet

Total time: 3 hrs 15 mins

Servings: 16

Ingredients:

- 1½ cup melted butter
- ½ cup powdered erythritol
- 1 cup coconut flakes
- ½ cup chopped almonds
- 2 tsp baking powder
- 4 egg whites

- 1 tbsp coconut extract
- ¼ tsp baking soda
- ¼ tsp salt
- 1¾ cup almond flour
- ½ cup goat milk yogurt
- ¼ cup olive oil

Directions:

Coat the crock pot with olive oil and line with parchment paper and then keep it aside.

Put melted butter in a pan and heat to bring the butter to a boil and cook till it turns golden brown in colour. Let the butter cool down a bit.

Mix almond flour, erythritol, baking soda, baking powder, and salt in a large mixing bowl and set it aside.

Combine the wet and dry mixtures together to make the batter for the bread. Pour the batter into the lined crock pot and cover it with a foil.

Cover the crock pot and cook on high setting for 2 hours 45 minutes. Check for the doneness of the bread and serve after complete cooling.

38. Super-Hot Chicken Omelette

Total time: 3 hrs 5 mins

Servings: 4

Ingredients:

- 1 cup milk
- 1 cup sharp cheddar cheese
- 8 eggs
- 1½ tsp hot sauce
- 1 cup cooked and shredded chicken
- Salt and black pepper

Directions:

Whisk the eggs in a bowl and add then all the other ingredients with the egg. Remember to season with salt and black pepper.

Coat the crock pot with olive oil and pour the egg mixture into it. Close the pot and cook on low setting for 3 hours. Let the omelette sit in the pot for some time and then open the lid.

Slice and garnish with some more cheese.

39. African Cuisine Chicken Curry

Total time: 4 hrs 30 mins

Servings: 6

Ingredients:

- 3 lb chicken breast, cubed
- 1 stalk of lemon grass, finely chopped
- 2 tsp minced ginger
- 5 cloves of garlic, minced
- 1 tsp turmeric
- 1 tbsp black pepper
- ½ tsp fenugreek seeds
- 2 tsp fennel seeds
- 1.5 tsp cumin powder
- 1.5 tsp mustard seeds
- 1.5 tsp red chilli flakes
- 1 tsp chilli powder
- 2 tsp salt
- 5 dried chillies, whole
- 2 cinnamon sticks
- ¼ cup apple cider vinegar
- 1 tbsp olive oil
- 1 tsp ground coriander
- 2 tbsp lemon juice
- 2 bay leaves

- ½ cup vegetable stock
- 1½ cup coconut milk
- 6 cardamom pods
- 8 curry leaves
- 1 cup reduced-lectin tomatoes, chopped
- 2 medium onions, sliced

Directions:

Heat a frying pan and roast all the spices and then grind them to make a smooth powder. Coat the chicken pieces with ginger, garlic, lemon juice, vinegar and powdered spices. Marinate the meat in the freezer overnight.

Now, heat olive oil in the crock pot and add the marinated chicken with tomatoes and coconut milk. Blend them well and cook without the lid for the first 30 minutes.

Now cover the crock pot and cook for another 4 hours, making sure that the chicken is tender.

40. Simple Buttery Peach

Total time: 3 hrs 5 mins

Servings: 8

Ingredients:

- 4 large peaches, thinly sliced
- 1 tsp liquid stevia
- 1 tsp cinnamon powder
- ¼ cup melted butter
- Salt

Directions:

Keep the peach slices aside and blend all the other ingredients in a bowl. Add the peach slices and toss them thoroughly to coat the peach slices. Put the coated peach slices inside the greased crock pot.

Cook on medium setting for 3 hours and then let the dish sit in the pot for some time.

Allow complete cooling before you serve.

41.Super Mango Sauce For Lectin Free Diet

Total time: 8 hrs 5 mins

Servings: 8

Ingredients:

- 2 cups ripe mango pulp
- 1 tsp cinnamon powder
- 1 tsp liquid stevia
- 1 cup water
- ¼ cup butter

Directions:

Keep all the ingredients in the crock pot and blend them thoroughly with a spatula.

Cook on medium setting for 8 hours. Let the sauce sit in the pot for some time and then remove the lid. Simmer the mixture for few more minutes to get the desired consistency.

Put the sauce in the blender and run the device to get the super creamy mango sauce.

42. Bundt Cake with Ripe Mango

Total time: 4 hrs 15 mins

Servings: 12

Ingredients:

- 1½ cups almond flour
- 1 tsp baking powder
- ½ tsp baking soda
- 1 cup cubed ripe mango
- ½ cup goat yogurt
- 1 tsp liquid stevia

Directions:

Mix the wet and dry ingredients separately and then mix them together to make the cake batter.

Pour the batter in the greased crock pot and remember to cover the lid with a couple of paper towels to prevent the dripping of moisture on the cake.

Bake on low setting for 4 hours and then let the cake sit in the pot for some time.

Cool down and serve chilled.

43. Broccoli Delight Omelette

Total time: 3 hrs 5 mins

Servings: 4

Ingredients:

- 1 cup milk
- 8 eggs
- 1 cup finely chopped broccoli florets
- 1 cup parmesan cheese
- Salt and pepper

Directions:

Keep the broccoli florets aside and put all the ingredients in a bowl and whisk hard to make a frothy mixture. Incorporate the broccoli florets and distribute them evenly in the egg mixture.

Coat the crock pot with olive oil and pour the egg mixture into it. Close the pot and cook on low setting for 3 hours. Open the lid immediately and serve by garnishing with more cheese.

44. Splendid Brussels Sprout Casserole For Lectin Free Diet

Total time: 8 hours 10 minutes

Servings: 8

Ingredients:

- 1 lb bacon
- 1 lb Brussels sprout, quartered
- 1 cup milk
- 1 tsp red chilli flakes
- 1 medium onion (diced)
- 8 oz shredded cheddar cheese
- 12 eggs
- 1.5 tbsp melted butter
- Salt and black pepper

Directions:

Cook the bacon in butter to make it crisp and then keep aside.

Coat the crock pot with butter and layer it with half portion of Brussels sprout at the bottom followed by half portions of onion, bacon and cheese. Repeat the layering and make sure that the top layer is made with cheese.

Beat the eggs and add milk with it and remember to season with salt and pepper.

Pour the egg mixture over the layers in the pot and cook for 8 hours on low setting.

Serve after topping with some more cheese.

45. Artichoke Hash For Lectin-Free Diet

Total time: 5 hrs 15 mins

Servings: 6

Ingredients:

- 1½ cups sliced onion
- ¼ cup vegetable broth
- 24 oz artichoke hearts, chopped
- ½ tsp dried thyme
- 1 tsp olive oil
- 1½ cups mushroom, chopped
- 1 cup gouda cheese, grated
- ½ cup mozzarella cheese
- 2 tsp fresh basil, chopped

Directions:

Grease and line the crock pot and keep it aside.

Heat olive oil in a large skillet and cook the artichoke hearts till they turn bright green in colour and then transfer them in a bowl. Use the leftover oil to cook the sliced onion and mushroom and make sure that they become light brown in colour.

Reserve the vegetable broth and mix all other ingredients (reserve the cheese for later use) with the cooked vegetables. Put this mixture into the lined crock pot and pour the broth over the top. Cover the pot and cook on low settings for 4 hours.

Now, open the lid and add the shredded cheese. Do not stir the contents in the pot and cover it again. Cook for one more hour and check if the cheese has melted completely.

Serve with grated cheese and basil.

46. Avocado Cobbler from Crock Pot

Total time: 6 hrs 10 mins

Servings: 4

Ingredients:

- 4 large avocados (sliced)
- 2½ cups baking mixture
- ½ cup milk
- 3 tbsp melted butter
- ½ tsp + ½ tsp stevia powder

Directions:

Make a mixture with avocados, ½ tsp stevia powder and ½ cup baking mixture. This will make the filling mixture for the cobbler.

Prepare the topping mixture by blending milk, ½ tsp stevia powder, butter and remaining portion of baking mixture.

Fill half portions of large size cupcake liners with the filling mixture followed by the topping mixture.

Place the place the filled cake liners inside the crock pot and then pour a cup of water in the pot. Use the medium setting and cook on high pressure for 6 hours. Let the cobblers sit in the pot for some time and then let them cool down completely before serving.

47.Buttery Apple Sauce (Lectin Free Diet)

Total time: 8 hrs 5 mins

Servings: 8

Ingredients:

- 1 tsp cinnamon powder
- 8 apples
- 1 cup water
- ¼ cup melted butter

Directions:

Cut the apples into dices and put all the ingredients in the crock pot and cook on medium setting for 8 hours. Let the sauce sit in the pot for some time and then remove the lid. Simmer the mixture for few more minutes if you think the mixture is too runny.

Put the entire mixture in a blender and run the device till you have the creamy sauce.

48. Healthy Spinach Omelette

Total time: 3 hrs 5 mins

Servings: 4

Ingredients:

- 1 cup milk
- 1 cup sharp cheddar cheese
- 8 eggs
- 4 cups baby spinach leaves
- Salt and black pepper

Directions:

Cook the spinach leaves with salt and water for 1 hour and then discard the water. Bring out the wilted spinach and keep them in a bowl. Put all the other ingredients in the bowl and whisk hard to make a frothy mixture. Remember to season with salt and black pepper.

Coat the crock pot with olive oil and pour the egg mixture into it. Close the pot and cook on low setting for 3 hours. Let the omelette sit in the pot for some time and then open the lid.

Slice the omelette into four slices and serve by garnishing with some more cheese.

49. Simple Crockpot Pudding

Total time: 4 hrs 5 mins

Servings: 4

Ingredients:

- 1 cup almond flour
- 1 tsp baking powder
- ½ cup butter
- 1 tsp liquid stevia
- 2 eggs
- ½ cup goat cream

Directions:

Blend butter and stevia in a bowl and then add the eggs with this mixture. Add the other ingredients one by one and let the mixture sit for a couple of minutes.

Coat the crock pot with butter and pour the mixture into the pot. Close the lid and cook on medium setting for 3 hours.

When the cooking time is up, let the pudding sit in the pot for some time and then open the lid. Allow complete cooling before putting the pudding in the fridge to chill.

50. Super Healthy Vegetable Casserole

Total time: 25 mins

Servings: 12

Ingredients:

- 2½ cups cooked spinach
- 1½ cups cooked mushroom
- 4 tbsp marinara sauce
- 8 eggs
- 2 cups milk
- 2 cups mozzarella cheese
- Salt and black pepper

Directions:

Line the crock pot with parchment paper and grease with butter. Spread the cooked spinach and mushroom (in layers) at the bottom followed by spreading the cheese on top.

Beat the eggs and whisk with milk, marinara sauce, salt and pepper. Pour this egg mixture over the vegetables and cheese in the pot. Cover the pot and cook on low setting for 3 hours.

Bring out the casserole dish along with the parchment paper and serve by slicing into desired sizes.

51.Crock Pot Peach Sauce

Total time: 8 hrs 5 mins

Servings: 8

Ingredients:

- 1 tsp cardamom powder
- 8 peaches
- 1 cup water
- ¼ cup melted butter
- A pinch of salt
- 1 tsp liquid stevia

Directions:

Cut the peaches in medium dices and put all the ingredients in the crock pot and cook on medium setting for 8 hours. Let the sauce sit in the pot for some time and then remove the lid. Simmer the mixture for few more minutes.

Use a blender to make the smooth and creamy sauce and serve after chilling.

52. Delicious Mango Pudding

Total time: 3 hrs 5 mins

Servings: 8

Ingredients:

- 2 cups milk
- ¼ cup butter
- 2 eggs
- ½ tsp stevia powder
- ½ cup mango pulp
- 10 slices of white bread

Directions:

Cut the bread in small cubes and keep aside.

Make a mixture with milk, mango pulp, butter, eggs and stevia in a bowl and then soak the bread cubes in this mixture. Put the soaked bread cubes along with the remaining liquid mixture in the greased crock pot.

Close the pot and cook on medium setting for 3 hours. Let the pudding sit in the pot for some time and then allow complete cooling.

Serve chilled.

53.Sauce-de-Lemon (Lectin Free Diet)

Total time: 8 hrs 5 mins

Servings: 8

Ingredients:

- 1 cup lemon pulp
- 1 tsp cinnamon powder
- 1 tsp liquid stevia
- ¼ cup melted butter
- 1 cup water

Directions:

Keep all the ingredients in the crock pot and blend them thoroughly with a spatula. Cook on medium setting for 8 hours. Let the sauce sit in the pot for some time and then remove the lid. Simmer the mixture for few more minutes if necessary.

Use an immersion blender to make smooth and creamy sauce.

54. Rich Nutty Cobbler (Crockpot Cooking)

Total time: 8 hrs 10 mins

Servings: 4

Ingredients:

- 3½ shredded coconut
- 2.5 cups baking mixture
- ½ cup milk
- 3 tbsp melted butter
- 1 tsp stevia powder
- ½ cup chopped pistachio nuts

Directions:

Blend the baking powder and baking soda and keep the mixture aside for later use.

Prepare the filling mixture by mixing coconut, half portion of stevia powder and ½ cup baking mixture.

Prepare the topping mixture by blending all the other ingredients.

Fill half portions of large size cupcake liners with the filling mixture followed by the topping mixture.

Place the place the filled cake liners inside the crock pot and then pour a cup of water in the pot. Use the medium setting and cook on high pressure for 6 hours. Let the cobblers sit in the pot for some time and then let them cool down completely.

Serve after garnishing with some chopped pistachio.

55.Splendid Pork With Apricot Flavour

Servings: 6

Total time: 7 hours 50 minutes

Ingredients:

- Salt
- Ground black pepper
- 2 tbsp packed brown sugar
- ½ cup bottled chilli sauce
- 3 lb pork ribs
- ½ cup apricot preserves
- 1 chipotle in abodo sauce

Directions:

Keep the broiler ready by preheating it.

Cut the pork ribs into small pieces and season with pepper and salt. Broil them for 10 minutes and make sure that they become brown in colour. Now keep them inside the crock pot.

Put the chilli sauce, brown sugar, apricot preserves and chilli peppers in a bowl and mix them well. Pour this mixture over the pork pieces inside the crock pot and cook by covering it on low setting for 7 hours.

When cooked, skim out the fat from the cooking juices and serve it with the pork as the sauce.

56. Delicious Ham Sandwich

Total time: 4 hours 15 minutes

Servings: 12

Ingredients:

- 2 cups of apple juice
- ½ cup sweet pickle relish
- 1 tsp paprika
- 12 white sandwich bread
- 2 tsp homemade mustard
- 3 lb ham (thinly sliced)
- ¾ tsp liquid stevia

Directions:

Separate the slices of ham and keep them in the crock pot.

Use a small bowl to mix the apple juice with stevia, mustard, paprika and relish and pour it over the ham. Cover the crock pot and cook on low setting for 4 hours.

Place a couple of ham slices in between the bread and serve with some more sweet relish.

57. Apple Flavoured Pork For Lectin Free Diet

Total time: 7 hours 10 minutes

Servings: 4

Ingredients:

- 3 lb pork pieces
- 1/8 tsp ground black pepper
- 1 tsp curry powder
- 2/3 cup homemade barbecue sauce (made from reduced-lectin tomatoes)
- 2 cups cooked Cauliflower noodles
- Chopped onions for garnishing
- 1 medium onion
- ¼ tsp salt
- 1 cup apple puree
- Chopped apples for garnishing

Directions:

Blend the apple puree with curry powder and barbeque sauce to make a smooth paste. Put pork pieces, black pepper, onion and salt in the crock pot and pour the apple paste over the meat.

Cover the pot and cook on low setting for 7 hours.

Transfer the pork pieces in serving plate and toss the juice with cooked cauliflower noodles and then serve by garnishing with finely chopped apples and green onion.

58. Super Apple Hotdog

Total time: 1 hour 10 minutes

Servings: 7

Ingredients:

- 8 oz prepared mustard
- 1 tbsp apple cider vinegar
- 2 cups homemade apple sauce
- 2 lb hot dogs
- 1/8 tsp stevia

Directions:

Blend vinegar, apple sauce, mustard and stevia to make a smooth paste.

Keep the hotdogs in the crock pot and pour the sauce mixture over them. Cover and cook on low setting for one hour.

Serve warm with white bread and vegetables.

59. Lectin Free Meat Balls

Total time: 1 hour 30 minutes

Servings: 16

Ingredients:

- 16 oz salsa
- 1 cup water
- 2 eggs
- 16 oz sausage
- 2 lb ground beef
- 1 small onion (chopped)

- 1 cup apple sauce
- 1 tbsp lemon juice
- 1 tsp ground black pepper
- ½ cup white bread crumbs
- 1 tsp salt

Directions:

Boil salted water in a pot (without the lid) and cook the sausages for 10 minutes in it. Drain the cooked sausage and then cut them into bite sized pieces.

Keep the sausage pieces in the crock pot and add salsa, lemon juice, apple sauce and water to it. Beat the eggs in a bowl and add the beef, salt, pepper, bread crumbs and onion. Blend them by hand and make small balls from the mixture. Keep the meat balls with the sausage pieces in the crock pot but do not stir.

Cook on low setting for an hour and stir well before serving.

60. Lectin Free Beef Brisket

Total time: 10 hours 25 minutes

Servings: 10

Ingredients:

- 3 lb boneless beef brisket
- ¼ cup chilli sauce
- 2 medium onions, sliced and separated into rings
- 1 bay leaf
- 1 clove minced garlic
- ½ tsp stevia powder
- ½ tsp dried thyme
- ¼ tsp salt
- ¼ tsp ground black pepper
- 2 tbsp cold water

Directions:

Mix bay leaf and onion with the meat piece and keep them in the crock pot and make the sauce in a separate bowl.

Put stevia, garlic, thyme, garlic, beer, chilli sauce, pepper and salt in a bowl to make the sauce and then pour the sauce over the meat in the pot. Cover the cooker and cook on low setting for 5 hours.

Take the meat to the serving plate along with onion rings and discard the bay leaf. Cut the meat along the grain and keep covered.

To make the gravy, skim off the fat from the cooking juices and keep 2½ cups of the juice (discarding the rest). Pour cold water in a saucepan to mix thoroughly and then pour the cooking juice to it. Cook on medium heat and keep stirring so that no lumps are created. When thick and bubbly, pour the gravy over the meat and onion.

61. Super Orange Pudding For Lectin Free Diet

Total time: 3 hrs 5 mins

Servings: 8

Ingredients:

- 2 cups milk
- 2 eggs
- ½ cup orange pulp
- ¼ cup butter
- ½ tsp liquid stevia
- 10 slices of white bread, cubed

Directions:

Blend milk, butter, orange pulp, eggs and stevia in a bowl and then soak the bread cubes in this mixture. Put the soaked bread cubes in the greased crock pot along with the remaining liquid mixture.

Close the pot and cook on medium setting for 3 hours. Let the pudding sit in the pot for some time and then put in the fridge to chill.

Serve chilled with homemade orange sauce.

62.Super Fishy Omelette

Total time: 5 hrs 5 mins

Servings: 4

Ingredients:

- 8 eggs
- 1 cup milk
- 1 cup sharp cheddar cheese
- 1 cup salmon cubes
- 1 tbsp lemon juice
- 1 tbsp melted butter

Directions:

Coat the fish cubes with lemon juice and marinate for an hour.

Now, heat butter in the crock pot and cook the salmon cubes for 2 hours. Now, bring out the fish cubes from the pot and keep them aside. Do not discard the remaining butter from the pot.

Beat the eggs in a bowl and add all the other ingredients with the egg. Remember to season eggs with salt and pepper. Add the cooked fish cubes and distribute them evenly in the egg mixture.

Pour the egg mixture into the crock pot and close the lid and cook on low setting for 3 hours. Let the omelette sit in the pot for some time and then open the lid.

Slice the omelette into four slices and serve by garnishing with some more cheese.

63. Ham'n'Greens – Super Healthy Combo

Total time: 6 hours 20 minutes

Servings: 10

Ingredients:

- 1 tsp red chilli flakes
- 1.5 lb fresh collard greens
- 4 cups water
- ¼ tsp salt
- 1 large onion (halved and sliced)
- 3 lb meaty ham bones
- ¼ tsp stevia

Directions:

Remove the stems from the collard greens and chop the leafy portions.

Place the ham bones along with all the other ingredients in the crock pot and top them with the chopped collard greens.

Cover the pot and cook on low setting for 6 hours.

When cooked, pick out the ham bones and when they become a bit cooler, cut off the meat and discard the bones. Chop the meat and stir them to the mixture in the crock pot.

Serve it warm in serving bowls.

64. Super Turkey Sandwich (Lectin Free Dish)

Time taken: 5 hours 15 minutes

Servings: 12

Ingredients:

- 1 cup chopped mushroom
- 6 lb turkey breast
- 1 onion (chopped)
- 4 tsp beef Bouillon granules
- ¼ cup chilli sauce
- 3 tbsp white vinegar
- 2 tbsp Italian seasoning
- 12 white sandwich buns (sliced)

Directions:

Keep the turkey meat in the crock pot and add the mushrooms and onion.

Mix the beef bouillon with chilli sauce, seasoning mix and vinegar and pour the mixture over the meat in the pot.

Cook by covering the pot for 5 hours on low setting.

Bring out the meat pieces from the pot and use forks to shred the meat. Take the shredded meat back to the pot and heat it thoroughly.

Prepare the sandwiches by placing spoonful of meat mixture in between each slices of bread.

65. Bliss Of Bacon Omelette

Total time: 3 hrs 5 mins

Servings: 4

Ingredients:

- 1 cup milk
- 2 medium bacon slices
- 1 cup parmesan cheese
- 8 eggs
- Salt and pepper

Directions:

Cook the bacon in the crock pot till they become very crispy. Bring them out from the pot and allow complete cooling. When cooled, crumble them by hands and keep aside. Do not discard the bacon grease from the crock pot.

Now, put all the other ingredients in a bowl and whisk hard to make a frothy mixture. Incorporate the bacon and distribute them evenly in the egg mixture.

Pour the egg mixture into the bacon greased crock pot and close the pot and cook on low setting for 3 hours. Open the lid immediately and serve by garnishing with more cheese.

66. Tasty Mushroom & Sausage Combo Sandwich

Total time: 4 hours 15 minutes

Servings: 10

Ingredients:

- 2 cups mushroom, chopped
- 48 oz pasta sauce
- 2 onions (sliced)
- ½ tsp crushed fennel seeds
- ½ tsp garlic powder
- 10 white sandwich bread, sliced
- 40 oz Italian turkey sausage

Directions:

Mix the mushroom with pasta sauce, onions, garlic powder and fennel seeds in the crock pot and cook on low setting for 4 hours.

Cook the sausages in the indoor grill and slice them along the length.

Place the sausages along with the cooked vegetables in between the buns and serve hot.

67.Lectin Free Pork Sandwich

Total time: 8 hours 15 minutes

Servings: 15

Ingredients:

- 1 envelope of onion soup mix
- 4 lb pork roast, cut into 2 pieces
- 1 cup sliced mushrooms
- 2 celery rib (finely chopped)
- 1 can of condensed cream of mushroom soup (undiluted)
- 15 hard rolls (split)

Directions:

Blend the onion soup mixture along with the mushroom soup and keep it aside.

Put the meat and celery in the crock pot and pour the soup mixture over the meat in the pot and cook by covering it on low setting for 8 hours.

When 30 minutes of cooking time is left, add the mushroom slices to the pot and continue cooking for the remaining time.

Bring out the meat from the pot and use forks to shred. Return the meat to the pot and heat up thoroughly.

Place the meat with the juices and vegetable in between the bread slices and serve.

68.Splendid Pork Ribs From Crockpot

Total time: 8 hours 40 minutes

Servings: 8

Ingredients:

- Lectin-free tomato puree
- ½ tsp stevia
- 4 lb pork ribs
- 1 cup chilli sauce
- 4 tbsp vinegar
- Salt and black pepper
- 2 tsp dried oregano
- 1 dash of hot sauce
- 2 tsp Worcestershire sauce

Directions:

Keep the oven ready by preheating at 400 degrees.

Preheat the oven at 400 degrees and season the pork ribs with pepper and salt and cook them in the oven for 30 minutes ensuring that the meat becomes brown on all sides. Remember to turn the meat after 15 minutes of cooking.

Mix all the other ingredients and add it in the crock pot along with the cooked pork.

Cover the pot and cook on low setting for 8 hours making sure that the meat becomes tender.

69.Sausage & Collard Soup

Total time: 8 hours 10 minutes

Servings: 6

Ingredients:

- 8 cups chicken broth
- Salt
- Black pepper
- 1 large onion, chopped
- ½ lb Andouille sausage links
- 1 tbsp red wine vinegar
- 2 stalks of celery, chopped
- 4 springs of fresh thyme
- 1 bunch of collard greens (cut into bite sized pieces)

Directions:

Keep the collard greens aside and put all other ingredients in the crock pot. Cover the pot and cook on low setting for 7 hours 30 minutes and then discard the thyme springs.

Now add the collard greens and cook for another 30 minutes, making sure that the collard greens are tender.

70. Super Broccoli Noodle Soup

Total time: 8 hours 30 minutes

Servings: 8

Ingredients:

- 1 lb ground beef
- 1 tbsp dried basil
- 3 cups beef broth
- 5 cloves of garlic, minced
- ¾ cup reduced-lectin tomato paste
- ¼ tsp pepper
- 1 cup water
- 1 tbsp dried parsley
- 1 cup vegetable stock
- ½ cup chopped onions
- 2 cups uncooked broccoli noodles
- 3 cups reduced-lectin tomatoes, diced
- Shredded cheddar cheese, for garnishing

Directions:

Blend the diced tomatoes with the tomato paste and pour the mixture into the crock pot.

Now add beef, broth, parsley, garlic, onion, basil, vegetable stock along with pepper and salt and mix them thoroughly.

Cover the pot and cook on low setting for 8 hours. Add a cup of water in the pot along with the broccoli noodles and cook them for another 30 minutes and serve with shredded cheese.

71.Soup With Tortellini (Crockpot Dish)

Total time: 7 hours 35 minutes

Servings: 6

Ingredients:

- 2 cups water
- 24 oz reduced-lectin tomato sauce
- 4 cloves of garlic, minced
- ¼ cup diced onion
- 1 lb ground beef, browned
- 4 cups beef broth
- 4 cups loosely packed spinach leaves
- ½ cup diced sweet potato
- 8 oz sliced fresh mushrooms
- 8 oz cream cheese, cut into 1 inch cubes
- 16 oz tortellini cheese

Directions:

Make a mixture with the tomato sauce, beef, water, garlic, onion, spinach, sweet potato, beef broth, cream cheese and mushrooms in the crock pot and cook on low setting for 7 hours.

Now whisk to break the chunks of cream cheese and then mix the tortellini cheese and stir well. Cover the cooker and cook for another 30 minutes and serve hot.

72. Cheesy Sweet Potato

Total time: 6 hours 45 minutes

Servings: 6

Ingredients:

- ½ cup chopped onions
- 2 tbsp butter
- 4 cups sweet potatoes, diced
- 1 cup water
- 1 cup milk
- 3 tbsp white flour
- 32 oz chicken broth
- ½ cup diced celery
- 4 green onions, sliced
- ¼ cup bacon pieces
- 8 oz shredded cheddar cheese

Directions:

Heat butter in the crock pot and mix the sweet potato dices with onion, chicken broth, celery and water in the crock pot and cover with a lid. Set on low and cook for 6 hours.

Pour the milk in a bowl and mix the flour in it. Pour this liquid over the cooked potatoes in the pot and increase the heat. Cook for 25 minutes by covering the pot and then stir in the shredded cheese. Cook for 5 more minutes, ensuring the cheese has melted completely.

Serve by seasoning with pepper and salt.

73. Broccoli & Ham Delight Soup

Total time: 7 hours 10 minutes

Servings: 12

Ingredients:

- 4 large broccoli heads
- 1 medium onion, diced
- 1 tsp thyme leaves
- Black Pepper
- ½ cup sour cream
- 2 tsp parsley
- 3 cups ham, diced
- salt
- 5 cups chicken broth
- 1 cup milk

Directions:

Reserve the milk and sour cream for later use.

Mix all the other ingredients in a crock pot. Cook them by covering the pot on low setting for 7 hours.

Now add the milk and sour cream and cook for 10 more minutes by frequent stirring.

Check the seasoning and serve the soup warm.

74. Delicious Taco Flavoured Beef Soup

Total time: 6 hours 10 minutes

Servings: 5

Ingredients:

- 1 garlic clove, minced
- 1 cup reduced-lectin tomatoes, diced
- 1 tbsp chopped green chillies
- 1 cup shredded cheddar cheese
- 10.75 oz condensed cheddar cheese soup
- 1 medium diced onion
- 1 lb ground beef
- 1 oz taco seasoning
- 1.5 cups milk

Directions:

Put the beef, garlic and onion in a skillet and cook till the meat turns uniformly brown. Drain off excess fat.

Put the cooked meat in the crock pot and add the remaining ingredients. Cover the pot and cook on low setting for 6 hours.

Stir well to blend all the ingredients and serve hot.

75. Majestic Orange Cobbler

Total time: 8 hrs 10 mins

Servings: 4

Ingredients:

- 3.5 cups orange pulp
- 2½ cups baking mixture
- Zest of ½ orange
- ½ cup milk
- 3 tbsp melted butter
- 1 tsp stevia powder (divided in 2 parts)

Directions:

Make a mixture with orange zest and pulp, half portion of stevia and ½ cup baking mixture. This will make the filling mixture for the cobbler.

Make the topping mixture by blending all the other ingredients.

Fill half portions of large size cupcake liners with the filling mixture followed by the topping mixture.

Place the place the filled cake liners inside the crock pot and then pour a cup of water in the pot. Use the medium setting and cook on high pressure for 6 hours. Let the cobblers sit in the pot for some time and then let them cool down completely.

Serve chilled.

76. Bacon Topped Cheesy Sweet Potato Soup

Total time: 8 hours 30 minutes

Servings: 10

Ingredients for making the soup:

- 7 cups chicken broth
- 4 lb sweet potato dices
- ¼ tsp black pepper
- 16 oz less fat cream cheese
- 5 cloves of garlic, chopped
- 1 white onion, diced

Ingredients for topping:

- Green onion
- Grated cheddar cheese
- Sour cream
- Cooked and crumbled bacon

Directions:

Put the sweet potato in the crock pot along with garlic, pepper, onion and chicken broth and cook on low setting for 8 hours.

Pour the soup in a blender to make smooth paste and add the topping ingredients and pulse a few seconds to blend the toppings thoroughly.

77. Reduced –Lectin Tomato Soup

Total time: 8 hours 45 minutes

Servings: 8

Ingredients:

- 1 tbsp dried basil
- 1 cup diced celery
- 1 tsp dried oregano
- 2 cups reduced-lectin tomatoes, diced
- 1 cup diced onion
- 1 bay leaf
- Salt
- Black pepper
- 4 tbsp butter
- ½ cup white flour
- 1 cup parmesan cheese
- 4 cups chicken broth
- 2 cups heavy whipping cream

Directions:

Put the tomatoes with the juices, celery, oregano, basil, bay leaf, onion and chicken broth into the crock pot and stir well to combine them well. Cook on low setting for 8 hours making sure that the vegetables are tender.

When 30 minutes of cooking time is left, melt the butter in a pan and whisk flour in it to make a roux. Whisk the mixture till it becomes brown in colour and then pour a cup of soup into the pan to temper the roux and avoid forming clumps.

Return the soup mixture to the crock pot and stir to mix well. Serve hot with white bread sticks.

78.Cobbler Magic – de- Mango

Total time: 8 hrs 10 mins

Servings: 4

Ingredients:

- 2½ cups baking mixture
- 2 cups ripe mango pulp
- ½ cup milk
- 3 tbsp melted butter
- 1 tsp stevia powder (divided)

Directions:

Make the filling mixture by blending mango pulp, half portion of stevia and ½ cup baking mixture.

Prepare the topping mixture by blending remaining portions of baking mixture, stevia, milk and butter.

Fill half portions of large size cupcake liners with the filling mixture followed by the topping mixture.

Place the place the filled cake liners inside the crock pot and then pour a cup of water in the pot. Use the medium setting and cook on high pressure for 6 hours. Let the cobblers sit in the pot for some time and then let them cool down completely.

Serve chilled by topping with freshly sliced ripe mangoes.

79. Super Creamy Chard Soup

Total time: 1 hour

Servings: 4

Ingredients:

- 1 lb sweet potato
- 3 Swiss chard stems, chopped
- 2 tbsp unsalted butter
- Salt and pepper
- 4.5 cups chicken broth
- ½ cup heavy cream
- 1 tbsp snipped chives

Directions:

Cook the sweet potato along with chard and a pinch of salt in the melted butter for 10 minutes.

Pour all other ingredients in the crock pot with the vegetables and cook on high heat for 55 minutes.

Allow the mixture to cool down a bit and then use a hand blender to make smooth paste.

Serve the soup by heating up thoroughly before serving.

80. Delicious Brussels Sprout Soup

Total time: 8 hours 15 minutes

Servings: 8

Ingredients:

- 1 lb Brussels sprout
- 5 cloves of garlic, chopped
- 1 cup chopped onion
- ¾ tsp kosher salt
- 2 lb smoked ham hocks, chopped
- 1 cup chopped celery
- 6 cups water
- ½ cup light sour cream
- 2 cups cubed sweet potato
- 1 bay leaf
- 1 tsp freshly ground black pepper

Directions:

Put all the ingredients in the crock pot along with enough water to cover them and then cover the pot to cook on low setting for 8 hours.

Now remove the ham hocks so that you can remove the meat from the bones. Discard the bones and return the meat to the pot. Remember to discard the bay leaf as well.

Let the soup cool down a bit and then use a hand blender to make smooth soup. Serve after warming up thoroughly.

81. Almond Flavoured Pancake For Breakfast

Total time: 1 hour 5 minutes

Servings: 6

Ingredients:

- 1 cup milk
- ½ tsp salt
- 4 tbsp melted butter
- 1 cup almond flour
- 6 eggs

Directions:

Blend milk, almond flour, eggs and salt in a large mixing bowl. Coat the crock pot with a bit of olive oil and melt the butter in it.

Pour the batter in it and cook by covering the cooker for 1 hour on high setting. Make sure that the pancake is puffed up and serve with lectin-free sauce.

82.Super Easy Spinach & Ham Frittata

Total time: 2 hours 5 minutes

Servings: 6

Ingredients:

- ¼ cup milk
- ½ cup goat milk yogurt
- ½ tsp thyme
- ½ tsp garlic powder
- 1 cup baby spinach
- ½ tsp onion powder
- 1 cup diced ham
- 6 large eggs
- Salt and black pepper
- 1/3 cup diced mushrooms
- 1 cup cheese (shredded)

Directions:

Keep pepper, salt, yogurt, milk, thyme, garlic powder and onion powder in a large mixing bowl and whisk hard to make a smooth paste.

Now, add the spinach and mushrooms along with cheese and ham.

Coat the crock pot with olive oil and pour the mixture into it. Cover and cook for 2 hours and serve after slicing into pieces.

83. Majestic Cheesy Sausage Casserole

Total time: 4 hours 15 minutes

Servings: 8

Ingredients:

- 1 lb ground pork sausage
- 32 oz sweet potato, grated
- 1½ cheddar cheese (grated)
- 1 tbsp Creole seasoning
- ½ cup sliced green onion
- ½ cup milk
- ½ tbsp black pepper
- ½ tbsp onion powder
- ½ tbsp garlic powder
- 1 cup Mozzarella cheese (grated)
- Olive oil
- 12 eggs (beaten)

Directions:

Heat one tablespoon of olive oil in a separate pan and cook the sausage with half portion of the seasoning blend for 10 minutes, making sure that the sausage becomes brown in colour.

Spray the crock pot with olive oil and then make a layer of half portions of sweet potato and sprinkle the seasoning mixture.

Now, make a layer of half portion of cooked sausage and top with cheese layer. Repeat the layering with the remaining ingredients and remember to make the top layer with cheese.

Blend the eggs with milk and remaining seasoning and pour over the top.

Cover the crock pot and cook for 4 hours on high setting and serve by garnishing with green onions.

84. Smoky Mushroom Casserole

Total time: 5 hours 40 minutes

Servings: 8

Ingredients:

- 10 cups of cubed white bread
- 9 eggs
- 2 tbsp butter
- 1 lb bacon (thick slices)
- 1 medium onion, chopped
- ¼ cup chopped parsley
- 8 oz sliced fresh mushrooms
- ½ tsp red chilli flakes
- 2 cups "half-n-half"
- 2 cups smoked cheddar cheese (shredded)

Directions:

Keep the oven ready by preheating at 300 degrees. Spread the bread cubes on a cookie sheet and bake them for 30 minutes and make sure that they become dry.

Melt butter in a skillet and cook the mushrooms in it for 5 minutes.

Beat the eggs and add the pepper flakes with half-n-half.

Reserve ¾ cup of cheese and mix the remaining with the egg mixture and then stir in the bacon, 2 tablespoon of parsley and onion into it.

Now, fold in the bread cubes and stir well to coat. Pour the mixture into the crock pot and cook by covering it on low setting for 5 hours.

Open the lid and top with remaining cheese and parsley and cook without the lid for 10 minutes, making sure that the cheese melts completely.

Serve warm.

85.Lectin Free Ham & Eggs

Total time: 4 hours 20 minutes

Servings: 8

Ingredients:

- ½ cup green onions (chopped)
- ½ tsp red chilli powder
- 2/3 cup of half-n-half
- 1 cup Gruyere cheese (shredded)
- 12 eggs
- 4 oz cheddar cheese (shredded)
- ½ tsp freshly ground black pepper
- 2 cups of cooked ham (cubed)
- ½ tsp salt
- 9 oz frozen spinach (thawed and drained)
- 6 cups sliced sweet potatoes

Directions:

Line the crock pot with a foil and coat it with olive oil.

Use a bowl to beat the eggs with salt, black pepper, half-n-half and red chilli powder. Keep aside ¾ cup of cheddar cheese and 2 tablespoons of green onions and mix them together in a separate bowl.

Layer half portion of sweet potatoes at the bottom of the lined crock pot followed by spinach, ham, green onions and cheese. Repeat the layering order and make the top layer with cheese. Pour the egg mixture over the top.

Cover the crock pot and cook on low setting for 4 hours ensuring the egg is properly set.

Garnish with remaining cheese and onion and serve warm.

86. Lectin-Free Super Spicy Tortillas

Total time: 4 hours 30 minutes

Servings: 8

Ingredients:

- 1 lb chorizo sausage
- 1 red onion, chopped
- 2 cups Pepper Jack cheese, shredded
- ¾ cup sliced green onions
- 1 jalapeno chilli, seeded and finely chopped
- 1½ cup milk
- 9 white flour tortillas
- 8 eggs
- 2 tbsp fresh cilantro, chopped
- 1 cup Old El Paso salsa

Directions:

Coat the crock pot with olive oil and keep 3 tortillas at the bottom. Tear them according to your requirement so that the bottom is well covered with the tortillas.

Blend the eggs with milk and keep aside. Reserve 2 tablespoon of onion and ¾ cup cheese.

Top the tortillas with half portion of sausage followed by layers of green onion, red onion and cheese and repeat the layers with remaining ingredients.

Top the layering with the remaining tortillas and then pour the egg mixture from top. Cover and cook on low setting for 4 hours making sure that the egg is set.

Sprinkle the reserved cheese and onions before serving.

87. Apricot Flavoured Super Pork

Total time: 8 hours 10 minutes

Servings: 4

Ingredients:

- 3 lb pork ribs
- 1 can chipotle pepper in abodo sauce
- 18 oz apricot preserve
- 2 medium onions, sliced and separated into rings
- 2 tbsp balsamic vinegar
- 1/3 cup apple juice
- Salt
- Black pepper

Directions:

Slice the onion and then separate them in rings.

Make the layer of onion rings at the bottom of the crock pot and then lay the pork pieces on top. Put chipotle pepper, apple juice and balsamic vinegar in a blender to make a smooth sauce. Pour it over the pork and cover the pot to cook for 8 hours on low setting.

Boil apricot preserve in a pan along with a pinch of salt. Cook till you have the desired consistency of the sauce. Serve the warm sauce with the pork.

88. Mango Flavoured Chicken Drumsticks

Total time: 8 hours

Servings: 4

Ingredients:

- 1/3 cup mango preserves
- 2½ lb chicken drumsticks
- 2 tsp yellow mustard
- Fresh ripe mango, diced
- 1 cup homemade barbecue sauce (made from reduced-lectin tomatoes)

Directions:

Put mango preserve, mustard, barbeque sauce and ripe mangoes in a bowl and use a hand blender to make smooth sauce.

Keep the chicken drumsticks in the crock pot and pour the sauce over the meat.

Cover the pot and cook on low setting for 8 hours. Serve by garnishing with the fresh mango cubes.

89. Super Tasty Taco Flavoured Chicken Soup

Total time: 6 hours 10 minutes

Servings: 5

Ingredients:

- 10 oz reduced-lectin tomatoes
- 1 tsp green chillies, chopped
- 2 cups chicken broth
- 1 clove of garlic, minced
- 1 cup shredded cheddar cheese
- 10.75 oz condensed cheddar cheese soup
- 1 medium diced onion
- 1 lb ground chicken
- 1 oz taco seasoning
- 1.5 cups milk

Directions:

Cook chicken in a skillet along with garlic and onion, till the meat turns completely brown. Drain off excess fat after cooking.

Put the cooked meat in the crock pot and add the remaining ingredients. Cover the pot and cook on low setting for 6 hours.

Stir thoroughly and serve hot.

90. Noodle & Turkey With Mango Sauce

Total time: 7 hours 10 minutes

Servings: 4

Ingredients:

- 3 lb turkey pieces
- 1 tsp curry powder
- 2/3 cup homemade barbecue sauce (made from reduced-lectin tomatoes)
- 1/8 tsp ground black pepper
- 2 cups cooked broccoli noodles
- Chopped onions
- 1 medium onion, chopped
- ¼ tsp salt
- ½ cup homemade mango chutney
- Chopped mango for garnishing

Directions:

Blend the mango chutney with curry powder and barbeque sauce to make a smooth paste. Put turkey meat, black pepper, onion and salt in the crock pot and pour the mango paste over the meat.

Cover the pot and cook on low setting for 7 hours.

Transfer the turkey pieces in serving plate and toss the juice with cooked broccoli noodles and then serve by garnishing with finely chopped mango and green onion.

91.Splendid Avocado Bread For Lectin-Free Diet

Total time: 3 hrs 5 mins

Servings: 16

Ingredients:

- 1¾ cup almond flour
- 1 tsp stevia powder
- 1 tsp ground nutmeg
- ¼ tsp baking soda
- 2 tsp baking powder
- ¼ cup Olive oil
- ½ cup apple juice
- 2 cups mashed avocado
- ½ cup goat milk yogurt
- 4 egg whites
- ¼ tsp sea salt
- 1 tbsp vanilla extract
- ¼ tsp ground allspice
- 2 oz chopped almonds

Directions:

Grease the crock pot with olive oil and then line it with parchment paper.

Put apple juice and mashed avocado in a pan and cook them on high heat to bring the mixture to a boil. Remove the pan from heat and then allow a bit of cooling.

Mix almond flour, stevia, baking soda, baking powder, ground allspice, nutmeg powder, and salt in a large mixing bowl and set it aside.

Add the apple mixture with vanilla extract, egg whites, yogurt, and olive oil and whisk hard to make a smooth mixture. Mix the wet and dry mixture thoroughly to make the smooth batter for the bread. Pour the batter into the greased crock pot and make the top smooth with the help of a spoon. Now, cover the top with a foil tightly.

Cover the crock pot and cook on high setting for 2 hours 45 minutes. Allow complete cooling before serving the bread.

92. Beef & Mushroom Blasting Hash

Total time: 6 hrs 15 mins

Servings: 6

Ingredients:

- 1 cup chopped mushroom
- 1½ cups sliced onion
- ½ tsp dried thyme
- 12 oz ground beef
- 1.5 lb baby spinach
- 1 tsp olive oil
- ¼ cup beef broth
- ½ cup shredded cheese
- 2 tsp fresh parsley, chopped

Directions:

Grease the crock pot with olive oil and line with parchment paper. Keep the pot aside.

Heat olive oil in a skillet and cook the beef till the meat is uniformly brown in colour. Remove the meat to a mixing bowl and use the leftover grease to cook the onion and mushroom. Cook them for few minutes and then bring them to the bowl with the cooked beef.

Reserve the broth and mix all the other ingredients with the cooked beef and vegetables. Put this mixture into the crock pot and spread the mixture evenly in the pot. Now, pour the beef broth over the top and cover the pot.

Cover the pot and cook on low setting for 6 hours.

Serve the hash after garnishing with shredded cheese and chopped parsley.

93.Utterly Butterly Spinach Frittata

Total time: 3 hrs 5 mins

Servings: 8

Ingredients:

- 14 oz fresh spinach leaves
- ¼ cup green onion, sliced
- 12 oz thinly sliced sweet potato
- ½ cup melted butter
- 8 eggs
- 4 oz feta cheese, crumbled

- ½ tsp red chilli flakes
- 2 tbsp parsley, chopped
- ¼ tsp ginger powder
- ¼ tsp garlic powder
- ¼ tsp allspice powder
- salt and black pepper

Directions:

Cook the spinach leaves with melted butter in a pan and make sure that the leaves wilt completely. Now pour the content in a large mixing bowl.

Place the sliced sweet potato at the bottom of the crock pot and then make the layer with sliced green onions. Put the eggs in the bowl of cooked spinach and add ground black pepper, chilli flakes, allspice powder, ginger powder, garlic powder and salt. Pour this mixture into the crock pot and use a fork to stir the contents gently. Make sure that the egg mixture is well distributed and the vegetables are well covered with it.

Cover the pot first with a foil and then with the lid. Cook on low setting for 3 hours and check for the doneness of the egg. Slice and serve after garnishing with parsley.

94. Chicken & Broccoli – Super Combo Hash

Total time: 5 hrs 15 mins

Servings: 6

Ingredients:

- 1½ cups sliced onion
- 1 large broccoli head, cut into small florets
- 1.5 lb shredded cabbage
- ½ tsp dried thyme
- ¼ cup chicken broth
- 8 oz minced chicken
- 1 tsp olive oil
- 2 tsp fresh basil, chopped
- 1 cup gouda cheese, grated
- ½ cup mozzarella cheese

Directions:

Grease the crock pot with olive oil and line it with parchment paper.

Heat olive oil in a large skillet and cook the broccoli florets till they turn bright green in colour and then transfer them in a bowl. Use the leftover oil to cook the sliced onion and make sure that they become light brown in colour. Add melted butter in the skillet to cook the minced chicken and season with salt.

Reserve the chicken broth and mozzarella cheese for later use. Put the cooked vegetables, onion, minced chicken and all other ingredient in a mixing bowl and blend them thoroughly. Pour this mixture into the lined crock pot and then pour the chicken broth from the top. Cover the pot and cook on low setting for 4 hours. Now, open the lid and add the mozzarella cheese on top. Cover the pot again and cook for one more hour. Make sure that the mozzarella cheese melts completely.

Serve the hash with some more cheese and basil.

95. Healthy Kale & Sweet Potato Stew

Total time: 3 hrs 5 mins

Servings: 4

Ingredients:

- 1 cinnamon stick
- ¼ tsp nutmeg
- 2 celery stalks, chopped
- 2 bay leaves
- 1 red onion, chopped
- 1 lb sweet potato, diced
- 2 lb baby spinach, roughly chopped
- Salt and black pepper
- 2 cups vegetable stock
- ½ cup heavy cream

Directions:

Keep onion, sweet potato, celery, cinnamon, nutmeg, bay leaves, spinach, vegetable stock, salt and pepper in the crock pot and cook on low setting for 3 hours. Make sure to cover the pot.

When 5 minutes of cooking time is left, add the cream and stir well. Cook for the remaining time without the lid and serve warm.

96. Thai Cuisine Chicken Curry

Total time: 3 hrs 30 mins

Servings: 5

Ingredients:

- 1 lb boneless chicken, cubed
- 2 cups coconut milk
- ½ cabbage head, finely shredded
- 1 medium onion, sliced
- 1 packet Thai curry paste
- 2 reduced-lectin tomato, diced
- 4 tbsp olive oil
- Salt and black pepper

Directions:

Heat the olive oil in the crock pot and cook the onion till they become light brown in colour. Now, add the tomato and cabbage and cook them for 5 minutes. Add the chicken and curry paste along with coconut milk and season according to necessity.

Cook without the lid for the first 20 minutes and then cover the crock pot and set it to low.

Cook for 3 hours on low setting and stir well.

97. Broccoli Curry With Sweet Coconut Flavour

Total time: 3 hrs 30 mins

Servings: 5

Ingredients:

- 1 large broccoli, cut into small florets
- 2 reduced-lectin tomatoes, grated
- 1 cup coconut milk
- 1 medium onion, sliced
- ½ cup shredded coconut
- 1 tsp chilli flakes
- 4 tbsp olive oil
- 3 tbsp ginger, grated
- 1.5 tsp minced ginger
- 1 tsp garam masala
- ½ cup coconut cream
- 1 tsp hot sauce
- 1 tsp turmeric

Directions:

Heat the olive oil in the crock pot and sauté onion, ginger and garlic till they become light brown and fragrant. Now, add broccoli florets, turmeric, coconut milk, chilli flakes, and hot sauce along with grated tomatoes. Stir them well and cook for next 20 minutes without covering the pot.

Cover the pot and cook on low setting for 3 hours. Open the lid and add the shredded coconut, garam masala and cream. Stir well and serve warm as a side dish.

98. Blissful Indian Chicken Curry

Total time: 3 hrs 30 mins

Servings: 6

Ingredients:

- 1 lb chicken thighs
- 1 cup coconut milk
- ½ cup heavy cream
- 1 tsp chilli flakes
- 3 tbsp ginger, minced
- 1.5 tsp minced ginger
- 1 medium onion, sliced
- 1 tsp turmeric
- 2 reduced-lectin tomatoes, grated
- 1 tsp hot sauce
- 4 tbsp olive oil
- 1 tsp garam masala

Directions:

Heat olive oil in a skillet and cook onion, garlic and ginger till they become translucent. Transfer them to the crock pot and add the chicken pieces along with turmeric, chilli flakes, coconut milk, tomatoes and hot sauce. Do not cover the pot and cook on low setting for 20 minutes.

Now, put on the lid and cook on low setting for 3 hours. Open the lid and then add the garam masala and heavy cream. Stir thoroughly and serve warm.

99. Power Chowder With Chicken & Mushroom

Total time: 6 hrs

Servings: 4

Ingredients:

- 1 lb chicken breast
- 6 oz button mushrooms, sliced
- 1 shallot, finely chopped
- 3 celery ribs, diced
- 4 cloves garlic, minced
- 1 lb bacon, crisped and crumbled
- 1 white onion, sliced
- 2 cups chicken stock
- 1 tsp thyme
- 4 tbsp melted butter
- 1 tsp garlic powder
- 8 oz cream cheese
- salt and black pepper

Directions:

Reserve butter for later use and put all the ingredients in a large mixing bowl. Coat the chicken pieces thoroughly in the spices and marinate in the freezer overnight.

Heat butter in the crock pot and put the marinated chicken in the pot. Cook without the lid for half an hour and then cover the pot. Cook on low setting for 5 hours and 30 minutes and check if the chicken is tender. Cook for some additional time if required. Serve warm.

100.   Lectin Free Beef Chilli

Total time: 6 hrs 15 mins

Servings: 8

Ingredients:

- 1 tbsp olive oil
- 2 lb grass-fed ground beef
- 4 garlic cloves, minced
- 1 onion, diced
- 3 celery ribs, diced
- 2 tbsp chilli powder
- 2 tsp ground cumin
- ¼ tsp ground cinnamon

- a pinch of ground clove
- 2 cups beef broth
- 3 oz pine nuts
- 15 oz sweet potato puree
- 1 tbsp adobo sauce from preserved chipotle
- 2 tsp red wine vinegar
- 2 tsp coconut aminos

Directions:

Heat one teaspoon oil in a skillet and cook the ground beef along with salt. Cook by breaking the meat chunks with a spatula and cook till the meat turns brown.

Pour in the remaining oil and add the garlic, onion and celery and cook them for 5 minutes. Now, add chilli powder, cumin, cinnamon and cloves and cook by stirring for a minute. Pour in the beef broth and scrape the bottom of the pan thoroughly. Pour this beef mixture into the crock pot.

Add nuts, sweet potato puree, adobo sauce, wine vinegar, coconut aminos and salt and pepper according to taste. Stir thoroughly with the spatula and then cover the crock pot. Cook on medium setting for 6 hours and serve the dish with chopped scallions and lime wedges.

CONCLUSION

We are happy to bring this book for you and hope that the recipes will bring sunshine in your life. We believe it is not at all easy to maintain any strict diet regime and also believe that it is the will power of our reader to make the impossible happen. We just want to make the journey easy with our humble effort of providing any kind of help (read getting the nice recipes for you here!!).

We are looking forward to bring more mouth-watering recipes for you in near future.

Happy cooking!